Ancients in Their Own
Greeks

Ancients in Their Own Words
Greeks

MICHAEL KERRIGAN

 Marshall Cavendish
Benchmark

Other Marshall Cavendish Offices:
Marshall Cavendish International (Asia) Private Limited, 1 New Industrial Road, Singapore 536196 • Marshall Cavendish International (Thailand) Co Ltd. 253 Asoke, 12th Flr, Sukhumvit 21 Road, Klongtoey Nua, Wattana, Bangkok 10110, Thailand • Marshall Cavendish (Malaysia) Sdn Bhd, Times Subang, Lot 46, Subang Hi-Tech Industrial Park, Batu Tiga, 40000 Shah Alam, Selangor Darul Ehsan, Malaysia

Marshall Cavendish is a trademark of Times Publishing Limited

All websites were available and accurate when this book was sent to press.

Library of Congress Cataloging-in-Publication Data

Kerrigan, Michael, 1959–
Greeks / by Michael Kerrigan.
p. cm. -- (Ancients in their own words)
Summary: "Offers insight into ancient times through the words of its peoples by featuring modern translations of some of the most important written records from ancient Greece, including: the Phaistos Disk; boundary stone of the Agora; the Aristotle Herma; and the Parian Marble, with examples of Greek lettering adapted from the Phoenician alphabet"--Provided by publisher.
Includes bibliographical references and index.

ISBN 978-1-60870-065-3

1. Greece--Civilization--To 146 B.C.--Juvenile literature. 2. Quotations, Greek--Translations into English--Juvenile literature. I. Title.

DF77.K465 2010
938--dc22

2009034429

Editorial and design by
Amber Books Ltd
Bradley's Close
74–77 White Lion Street
London N1 9PF
United Kingdom
www.amberbooks.co.uk

Project Editor: Michael Spilling
Design: Joe Conneally
Picture research: Natascha Spargo

For Marshall Cavendish Corporation:
Editor: Deborah Grahame
Publisher: Michelle Bisson
Art Director: Anahid Hamparian

CONTENTS

INTRODUCTION

IN GREECE, SIGNS OF HUMAN SETTLEMENT DATE BACK TO 5000 BCE.
But archaeologists believe the ancestors of the people we know
of as the Greeks came here from western Asia around 2000 BCE.

By that time, civilization was already flourishing on the southern island of Crete. For example, the Minoan culture had appeared around 2600 BCE. After a thousand years, however, it vanished abruptly from the archaeological record, swept away by some disaster. The Mycenaeans, who lived on the Greek mainland, modeled their culture on the Minoans. But their society, too, came to a catastrophic end. In the time that followed, scattered communities lived under the protection of warrior chieftains, whose hilltop strongholds became power centers.

People Power

By 800 BCE, a new type of polis (city-state) was springing up. Wealthy local lords wanted luxuries, and so craftsmen and merchants emerged to serve this need. Phoenician traders brought goods to Greece from ports around the Mediterranean. They also brought an alphabet, which the Greeks adapted to their own language. As the people prospered, they grew in confidence and independence, and, as a result, the center of power in the polis expanded. Eventually, the city itself grew more important than the ruling elite. The acropolis (the hill on which the lords had lived) became a ceremonial center, sacred to the city itself. The lord himself no longer decided what took place in the polis. Now, the general public discussed such decisions, in an early form of politics. This sort of civic activity reached its height in fifth-century Athens. Government by the people—democracy—introduced a glittering age of achievement in philosophy, literature, art, and science.

Democratic Decline

Competition between the cities produced prosperity at first. But eventually it brought destructive conflict. Athens and its rival Sparta were badly weakened by their long wars. King Philip II of Macedon (reigned from 359 to 336 BCE) reduced the Greek states to subject status. Under his son, Alexander the Great (reigned from 336 to 323 BCE), huge territories were conquered in Egypt and Asia in the name of Greece. But Greece itself became a backwater in this vast empire.

◀ Delphi was both the site of ancient Greece's most important oracle as well as the sacred Temple of Apollo (pictured). The Greeks believed Apollo killed the Python on this site, a deity who protected the center of the earth.

THE PHAISTOS DISK

WE HAVE NO IDEA WHAT IT WAS FOR, AND WE CANNOT TRANSLATE ITS TEXT, BUT THE PHAISTOS DISK STILL SPEAKS TO US OF A MAGNIFICENT MINOAN CULTURE.

Minos was a mythical king of Crete, a large island in the eastern Mediterranean. In a labyrinth (maze) under his palace, he was said to have kept the monstrous Minotaur. This terrifying beast was a man with the head of a bull. It ate youths and maidens sent by cities the king had conquered.

At the end of the nineteenth century, English archaeologist Arthur Evans (1851–1941) made a spectacular discovery at Knossos on Crete's northern coast. Here, he claimed, were the remains of the capital Minos had built. It was as splendid as anything in ancient legend. There was even a labyrinth of passages in the basement, though it seemed to have been used for storing huge quantities of food and drink.

Palace of Peace

Evans had unearthed a previously unknown civilization. He named it Minoan after King Minos. But while there were traces of the Minotaur story in the images of bull's heads that appeared everywhere, there was no sign of any monster. There was plenty of evidence of luxury and refinement. For example, Evans found lavish wall paintings.

◄ By modern standards, Arthur Evans's excavations at Knossos were a little too creative. Some experts believe he interpreted his findings to match the stories he already had in his head.

THE INSCRIPTION

WHAT DOES IT MEAN?
All we can really say about the incomprehensible symbols on the Phaistos Disk is that they highlight for us how little we know about the Minoan world.

Minoan scribes kept careful records but scholars have yet to decipher their meaning. At first, they wrote in a hieroglyphic script, using picture symbols in the way the Egyptians had done. Later they moved to what seems to have been an alphabetical form with different symbols for the different sounds. Modern researchers call this script "Linear A," but they have not had any better luck in trying to figure out what it meant.

▶ The Phaistos Disk has 241 characters, with forty-five different signs. The meaning of some, such as the fish, flowers, and birds, seem as though they really should be obvious. But just what do they mean?

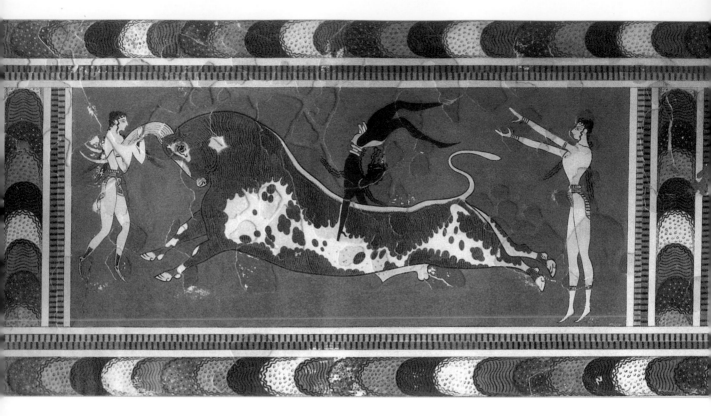

▲ In this mural found on the walls at Knossos, a youth appears to be vaulting over the back of a charging bull.

Some showed shapely male and female athletes vaulting over the backs of charging bulls, displaying grace and elegance triumphing over brute force.

Evans concluded that this society had been a matriarchy, which meant it was ruled by women. Statues of naked women were found, which he thought were symbols of female fertility and motherly love.

Paintings on walls and vases showed the Minoans had a deep love of nature, too. Knossos had no defensive walls, which seemed to indicate there was no threat of war or fear of being attacked by hostile neighbors.

A Modern Myth?

The conclusions Evans drew may have been a little fanciful. The existence of some statues of priestesses unclad above the waist for special ceremonies hardly proves that Minoan society was dedicated to free love. And the absence of walls does not necessarily mean that the Minoans lived peacefully. They lived on an island, so it is possible they would have defended themselves at sea.

Perhaps Evans was accidentally adding to the mythology that already surrounded the Minoans because, in fact, in the 1980s, archaeologists discovered that this civilization of peace and love had actually practiced human sacrifice. But Evans was right about the dominant status of women—or at least of some women—in

the form of a select few priestesses serving
Potnia, the earth goddess.

Mysterious Emblem

The ceramic disk found at Phaistos in
southern Crete in 1908 underlines how
little we really know of the Minoans.
Archaeologists have no idea what it was,
or what it was used for and, as yet, no one
can translate the script that spirals around
its face. (Instead of being inscribed, the
lettering had been stamped in the wet
clay before it was baked to hardness.)
To make matters more difficult, the
writing bears no resemblance to other
known scripts, even Minoan ones.
The answers to all these mysteries

disappeared with Minoan civilization
itself. Around 1500 BCE, the society
abruptly vanished. It is believed that
floating ash from the eruption of the
volcanic island of Thera (also called
Santorini) may have blotted out the sun,
creating a deep and disastrous winter
across the eastern Mediterranean.

▼ Evans assumed that a palace might actually have
been a temple complex, to which food and crops
were brought by farmers as a form of tax.

MYCENAE AND ITS MYSTERIES

EVEN THOUGH THEY WROTE IN WHAT IS CLEARLY AN EARLY FORM OF GREEK, THE MYCENAEANS OF MAINLAND GREECE ARE ALMOST AS MYSTERIOUS AS CRETE'S MINOANS.

Heinrich Schliemann (1822–1890) did for Mycenae what Arthur Evans did for Knossos—he discovered a spectacular civilization there.

Like Evans, though, he did not just find Mycenae, but also helped to shape the way people understood it. Homer's Iliad, the epic poem that tells the story of the War of Troy, had inspired Schliemann, so he was looking for a race of warrior heroes. And, among the ruins of Mycenae, he found what he was looking for.

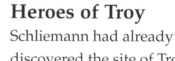

Heroes of Troy

Schliemann had already discovered the site of Troy in 1868, on the northwestern coast of Turkey. His rough-and-ready excavations there have horrified archaeologists. He dug straight down, destroying successive layers, until he reached what he considered to be the important layer. He did the same at Mycenae, in the Peloponnese (southwest of Athens), where he started digging in 1876.

He was not a man to stop and think or to pay

▲ Schliemann did a great deal of damage to the sites he dug, but he helped millions to see the romance of archaeology.

THE INSCRIPTION

WHAT DOES IT MEAN?

Scholars have only half translated the Mycenaeans' script. We can understand the nouns, which describe all the things they took such careful records of. However, we do not know what they did or how they felt.

The Mycenaeans' script, called "Linear B" by scholars today, was similar to the script used by the Minoans in some ways, but not in others. One of the differences was that, as scholars eventually figured out in the 1950s, it was in an early form of Greek. In theory, having understood this, researchers should have been able to read Mycenaean easily. The trouble was that the scribes kept their records in such brief note form (without a proper sentence structure or even verbs) that it is only possible to understand little snatches of what they wrote.

▼ This tablet was found in the Palace of Nestor in Pylos. The Mycenaeans' "Linear B" was obviously copied from the "Linear A" script used by the Minoans, but the characters stood for different things.

Much of what we know about Mycenae comes from a collection of ceramic tablets found at Pylos. But these were never meant to be a lasting record. Instead, they were soft-clay jotting pads for making quick notes. They would probably have been wiped clean and used again every day or so. Ironically, this collection was baked to hardness some three thousand years ago by the same fire that swept through Pylos, forever destroying this ancient city.

attention to solid facts that did not line up with his own theories. He was convinced that the Mycenaeans had been warriors who lived to fight.

Excavating earlier, in the 1840s, the Greek archaeologist Kyriakos Pittakis (1798–1863) had uncovered massive masonry walls and an impressive gateway, the Lion Gate. It is easy to see why Schliemann saw this as the

▼ The Lion Gate leading to the main settlement of Mycenae could only be the entrance to a great city, so Schliemann took it for granted that Mycenae had been a military power.

headquarters of a mighty, militaristic culture.

Now archaeologists know that the reality was rather different. Mycenae appears to have arisen at the start of the thirteenth century BCE, which was not long after the collapse of Minoan civilization. It seems that when the Minoan culture fell, a mainland state copied the Minoan economic system and adapted its written script for its own use. Inscribed ceramic tablets found at another Mycenaean city, Pylos, in southwestern Greece, have helped archaeologists piece together something of the story.

An Army of Officials

Mycenae did have an army, but it was more interested in making records than in making war. An army of scribes organized Mycenae's busy trading economy down to the tiniest detail. They tracked every shipment in and out of Mycenae's ports, and all the revenues and expenses of the state treasuries. For example, there are records detailing a single sheep sent by a small farmer to pay his tax, a cargo of bronze, and the fig and wheat rations paid to

▼ As this beautiful artifact shows, the Mycenaeans were every bit as artistic as the Minoans, and shared their fascination with the figure of the bull.

Pylos's thirty-seven female baths attendants. According to these records, one craftsman dedicated his working life to making blue-glass paste for jewelry, and another worked full-time making chariot wheels. There are entries for shepherds, woodcutters, and huntsmen, and women who worked as weavers, spinners, and corn-grinders.

15

KLEOMBROTOS, THE CHAMPION

A BRONZE TABLET, DISCOVERED AT THE SITE OF A FORMER GREEK COLONY IN CALABRIA, ITALY, HONORS AN OLYMPIC CHAMPION FROM THE SIXTH CENTURY BCE.

The city of Sybaris is found in Italy at the northwestern corner of the Gulf of Tarento, in what is now Cosenza. If Italy is shaped like a boot, then Sybaris is located in the toe. But in the sixth century BCE, the people living in Sybaris were Greek. Most had come from Helice, in Achaea, on the northern side of the Peloponnese. This was by no means unusual. At this time, there were Greek colonies the length and breadth of the Mediterranean and around the coasts of the Black Sea. Sybaris had been established quite early, around 720 BCE.

Greeks Abroad

This was a long time before the great classical city-states of Athens, Sparta, and Corinth had reached their height. None of the Greek cities actually had much power at this time, so it seems odd that they should have set up colonies. For example, Rome was a great power in Italy when it started expanding, and Britain was the world's

THE TRANSLATION

WHAT DOES IT MEAN?

Kleombrotos's dedication reminds us that the gods and goddesses were more than just myths to the Greeks, and that they would seek divine support in all their endeavors.

66 Kleombrotos son of Dexilaos, having won at Olympia and promised the prize to Athena, dedicated a tithe. 99

▼ Kleombrotos's plaque is crudely inscribed and the lines are not very tidy. However, the goddess (or her priests) would surely have been grateful for his gift.

17

◀ Unlike their modern equivalent, the ancient Olympics had a permanent home. The games were always held at Olympia, in the west of the Peloponnese, in southern Greece.

leading industrial nation when it built its empire in the nineteenth century. The United States, too, was considered the world's greatest democracy when it began extending its influence across the globe.

▶ Athena is most famous as the patron-goddess of Athens, but she was revered across the Greek world for her wisdom, handiwork, and warlike prowess.

In fact, the colonialism of the Greeks was prompted by the fact that they had so little at home. By sending out settlers to establish distant stations, the Greeks were able to secure much-needed resources. This also enabled them to promote their own industries and culture, and they exported fine ceramics and other luxuries.

The colonies, which kept in touch both with one another and with the mother country, were known as Magna Graecia (Greater Greece), and Sybaris belonged to this group. Instead of worshiping Italian gods, the Greeks of Sybaris built a temple to the goddess Athena, and they sent their top athletes to complete in the Olympic Games in Greece.

The Original Olympics

The Olympic Games were held every four years at Olympia, which is where they get their name. They had

first been staged as long ago as 776 BCE. All the Greek cities sent their finest athletes to compete in a range of events, including wrestling, boxing, running, the long jump, and javelin- and discus-throwing. Only young men competed (women were more or less completely excluded from Greek public life) and a great deal of pride and patriotism was at stake. The Greek cities were extremely competitive with one another, and every city wanted to outdo its neighbors if it could.

It was supposed to be an amateur event. The victor's prize was a wreath of laurel leaves. In theory, only honor was at stake, but with so much riding on the result, cities started to offer their athletes financial rewards. By the sixth century BCE, Athens is said to have been offering its athletes 500 drachmas for a win (about one million dollars in today's money).

An Offering of Thanks

This would explain why, when Kleombrotos came back a winner, he

▲ Staged regularly for more than a thousand years, the Olympics were seen as a showcase for the beauty, strength, and athleticism of Greece's youth.

dedicated a tithe (one-tenth) of his prize to the temple of Athena. One-tenth of a laurel wreath would obviously have been no use to anyone, but Athena (or at least her priests) could have always used a financial gift. The temple stood on the hill now known as the Timpone Motta, but twenty-six centuries ago it was the acropolis (raised area) on which the citadel of Sybaris, and its sacred center, stood. What remained of Athena's temple was excavated in 1963, and it was here that the tablet Kleombrotos had left behind was discovered.

DID YOU KNOW?

The city of Sybaris was famous throughout the ancient Greek world for its enormous wealth and the luxuries its leading citizens enjoyed. That reputation gave us a modern word, a sybarite, who is somebody who lives for pleasure.

19

HERE LIES ARCHILOCHUS

A MEMORIAL FIT FOR A HERO MARKS THE GRAVE OF A GREEK POET.
ARCHILOCHUS WAS A SOLDIER, BUT HE WAS ALSO A SATIRIST.

At first, Archilochus's grave on the Greek island of Paros had no memorial. According to the legend, it did not need it. You could always tell where he was buried, it was said, because of the wasps swarming above. Archilochus had a stinging satiric wit, and the wasps

▼ Paros is famous for its marble. This is used on the island itself, in this fine temple of Athena and, of course, in Archilochus's memorial.

were a reminder of just how painful his poetic jabs could be.

Archilochus was one of the very first ancient poets we know of. He was born in about 680 BCE, but was not the first Greek poet, of course. The *Iliad* and the *Odyssey*, which were the great epics of Homer, are thought to have been composed during the ninth century BCE. (That is, if any such single person as

Homer actually existed. Some scholars think the stories attributed to Homer were probably more likely to be stories passed on in the oral tradition that were eventually written down.) Around 700 BCE, Hesiod, another Greek poet, wrote pastoral poems and philosophical verses.

However, Archilochus was a very early poet, and he certainly developed something new. His verses were less formal than those that went before, and they were more personal. Where Homer and Hesiod had gone for grandeur, Archilochus wrote informally in what might have been his speaking voice.

THE TRANSLATION

66 Archilochus of Paros lies here; this monument was dedicated by Dokimos son of Neokreon. **99**

WHAT DOES IT MEAN?
The building of the memorial, seventy years after its subject's death, shows a growing pride in Greece's artistic achievements, even those of a prickly, mocking talent like that of Archilochus.

▲ Controversial as his reputation was, Archilochus received the sort of simple, dignified memorial that was traditionally given to a heroic warrior.

DID YOU KNOW?

Archilochus wrote what is thought to have been the first fable featuring animals. Typical of his poetry, it is brief and to the point:

The fox has many tricks;
The hedgehog only has one —
but it is a good one.

He was chatty, and at times even cheeky. He became famous as a master of the snappy insult. Along with scathing satirical attacks on his enemies, he also

▼ In this vase painting, the sun god Apollo rides his flaming chariot across the sky. He was also the god of medicine, music, and poetry.

wrote love poetry. This, too, tends to be light and humorous, though, rather than romantic or passionate. And even when he wrote about war, his enemies said, he did not take his subject as seriously as he should. After all, this was an age when war was seen as the highest and noblest of subjects.

A Legendary Talent

Archilochus was evidently a larger-than-life individual. Legends surrounded him even in his own lifetime. One said that he had fallen in love with a young lady named Neoubulé, whose father was one of the leading nobles of Paros. He had promised his daughter to the young poet,

but had then abruptly gone back on his word and refused the marriage. Archilochus, enraged, wrote a series of devastating satires that drove both the nobleman and his daughter to suicide.

Archilochus, with nothing to live for now, went off to live the life of a wandering soldier for hire. When Archilochus eventually died in battle, Apollo (the Greek god of poetry, as well as the sun) was said to have cursed the man who killed him.

A Sting in the Tail

While he had been alive, Archilochus had made himself a great many enemies in Paros. His countrymen cannot have been too sad to see him go. Over time, though, the sting of his satires lost its venom and the fame of his poetry grew. People in Paros could see that he had brought their island fame. And so, in 510 BCE, a simple column and slab-memorial

were placed on his grave, making it into a heroon (a hero's shrine).

As a satirist, Archilochus would surely have been amused to hear himself hailed a hero. He would also almost certainly have had a sarcastic thing or two to say about the way the otherwise unknown "Dokimos, son of Neokreon" used his memorial to memorialize himself!

▶ Homer wrote two great Greek epics. One is the *Iliad*, which tells the story of the Trojan War, and the other is the *Odyssey*, which describes the adventures of the hero Odysseus.

23

THE ATHENIAN AGORA

ATHENS WAS THE FIRST DEMOCRACY IN THE HISTORY OF THE WORLD.
AT ITS CENTER, ATHENS HAD A PLACE FOR PUBLIC ASSEMBLIES KNOWN
AS THE AGORA.

The Athenian agora was nothing much to look at—it was just an open space. Men came here at odd times of day to meet their friends and chat. They gossiped and talked about business or politics. Around the agora were stoai (covered walkways), their roofs held up by columns. Citizens could stroll through these stoai, sheltered from the sun or rain. Peddlers, acrobats, and other entertainers crowded in, too, and along the outer edge there were barbershops and bars. Beyond them, around the agora, were public buildings, such as law courts and the Athenian Assembly.

Why should such a place have been seen as sacred, then? There were splendid temples on the acropolis (hill) above the city, which was once the stronghold of

▼ The Parthenon (pictured) stands proudly on the acropolis, advertising Athenian prestige, but the focus of civic life was in the agora, below the grand temple.

WHAT DOES IT MEAN?

The roughly carved *horoi* stones not only defined the physical limits of the agora, but also marked out the public center of the city as a special, sacred space.

❝ I am the boundary of the agora. **❞**

◄ This simple stone marked out the heart of public life in the historic birthplace of "people power." It was Athens that first gave democracy to the world.

▼ Hermes, the messenger of the gods, also had responsibility for boundaries, which explains the hermae at the agora's northwestern corner.

the elite rulers of the city. Now, the focus of life had shifted to the area below. The Greek statesman Pericles (495–429 BCE) had built a beautiful complex on the acropolis known as the Temple of Athena, but also called the Parthenon, and it was only one of several stunning shrines. They could be seen from far out at sea, and were famed throughout the ancient world. Yet to the Athenians the temples and shrines were never as important as the agora.

Sacred to Democracy

Athens was the world's first democracy and the agora was prized precisely because it was where the citizens of Athens came together. The Athenians held their civic virtues with great reverence. The deity they worshiped above all others was Athena, patron goddess of their city. They took the sanctity of the agora seriously. No one who had committed a "crime of honor" was allowed to enter. These were crimes that might threaten the civic or social order, such as draft dodging or desertion from the army, the abuse of parents, or blasphemy (the abuse of the gods). In order to prevent any guilty man from straying into the agora, its boundaries were marked with *horoi* (roughly carved stones). There were also basins at the edge of the agora

▶ A general of genius, Alcibiades had a love–hate relationship with his home city. He became its greatest enemy and then, finally, its savior.

that enabled those about to enter to wash their hands, ritually cleansing them before they entered this sacred space.

The Hero and the Hermae

The northwestern corner of the agora had different boundary stones called hermae. They were flat stelae (stone monuments) each topped with Hermes's head. Hermes, the messenger of the gods, was also the god of boundaries, perhaps because his winged sandals carried him across them so effortlessly.

One morning in 415 BCE, the Athenians awoke to find that the hermae had been vandalized in the night. At that time Athens was bogged down in the Peloponnesian War (431–404 BCE) with Sparta, and an expedition was about to be sent to Sicily. Its leader was to have been Alcibiades (c. 450–404 BCE), who was a charismatic general. However, his popularity had upset the leading citizens of Athens, so they were quick to blame him for the damage to the hermae.

Alcibiades had already set off for Sicily when the order for his arrest went out. He knew he was not going to receive a fair trial, so he fled and the Sicilian expedition failed without him. Alcibiades went over to Sparta for a while, though he eventually came back and helped his home city's forces fight the Spartans until they sought to make peace with Athens.

THE WRITING ON THE WALL: GORTYN

AT GORTYN, A CITY-STATE IN SOUTHERN CRETE, THE ENTIRE LEGAL CODE WAS CAREFULLY INSCRIBED ON A WALL FOR ALL CITIZENS TO SEE.

The establishing of democracy is one of the great glories of Greece. But not all the Greek cities had advanced as far as Athens. Yet even where they had not got as far as introducing full democracy, the civic spirit was clearly very strong.

Gortyn, a city-state in the south of Crete, is a good example. The rule of law was so important to the people here that they had the whole legal code inscribed into a wall on public display.

The wall was built in about 450 BCE, and was part of a building that stood next to the agora, the city's central public space. It would have been logical if this building had been the city's *bouleterion* (council chamber) or the courthouse, which would seem a sensible place to put an

▼ Despite huge gaps, the Gortyn Code is the fullest statement we have of the kind of laws in force in Greece during the fifth century BCE.

THE TRANSLATION

WHAT DOES IT MEAN?
By displaying their law code for everyone to see, the people of Gortyn were making a statement about how important law and civic order were to them.

66 When a husband and wife are divorced, the wife is to have whatever property she brought with her to the marriage, as well as half of her income, if it is from her own property. Half the value of any cloth she has woven is hers as well, plus five staters [gold coins] if her husband has sent her away. If her husband denies that, then a judge has to decide.

If a slave going to a free woman should marry her, the children will be born free; but if the free woman goes to the slave, their children will be slaves. And if the same mother has both free and slave children, if she should then die her property would go to the free children.

A woman who gives birth to a child after leaving her husband having been divorced, she must have it taken to the husband's house before three witnesses. If he will not accept the child, it will be her right to decide whether to bring it up... 99

▼ Archaeologists put the surviving pieces of the wall together like a jigsaw puzzle. As a result, six hundred lines have been reconstructed, but much of the code has not been found.

Curiously, the Gortyn Code is written in a style known as boustrophedon (which means turning like an ox). In early Greek script, the writer began working from left to right. When he got to the end of a line, instead of jumping back to the left-hand side to start again, he simply dropped a line and started working his way back from right to left, just like a plowing ox when it reached the end of a furrow.

inscription of this kind. But we have no way of knowing if this was actually the case. Very little of the wall has survived because Greek (and then later Roman) builders took the stones.

Every Eventuality

What remains of the Gortyn Code covers an area of wall 30 feet (9 meters) across and about 5 feet (1.5 m) high. There are about six hundred lines of

text, all apparently inscribed by a single hand. Some deal with business and trading laws, but most are about family issues, such as marriage, divorce, and the various rights and duties of parents and children. There must have been a big section on criminal law as well, but this has never been discovered.

The code has something to say about just about every aspect of home life, from the rules of inheritance to the rights of slaves. The idea seems to have been to anticipate every possible legal problem that might arise. A detailed code of laws, set out in public for everyone to see, would allow disagreements to be resolved and disputes avoided.

▼ Over many centuries the Gortyn Wall was mostly broken up to use as building materials. Many of its stones found their way into the structure of a concert arena of the Roman era.

DEMOCRATIC JUSTICE

ATHENIAN DEMOCRACY DID NOT JUST INVOLVE BIG DECISIONS AND THE GOVERNMENT OF THE STATE; IT EXTENDED TO THE AREA OF JUSTICE, TOO.

The real importance of these voting disks is the raised bump in the center. In some it is solid while in others it is a hollow tube. If you put your finger over the end of the raised bump as you held the disk, no one would ever know which kind it was. Each of these cast-iron ballots represented a jury member's secret vote.

As they entered the court to hear the trial, each juror would be given two disks, one of each type. The one with the solid bump represented a vote in favor of the defendant, meaning "not guilty." The hollowed-out bump was a vote for the plaintiff (the person bringing the court action) or the prosecutor, and using it would mean the jury member thought the defendant was guilty as charged.

Voting a Verdict

As the jury filed out of the court at the end of the case, they passed a pair of urns (huge jars). One was for chosen ballots. The other was for rejected ones. Each juror would be holding a ballot in each hand, so no one could see which type of disk he was using to cast his vote. Once everybody had made his decision, the guilty and not guilty ballots in the first urn were counted and the verdict of the court was established.

◀ The law courts were situated beside the agora at the heart of the city. The administration of justice was central to Athenian life.

WHAT DOES IT MEAN?

The development of these ballots shows how seriously the Greeks took their democratic duties, and how important they believed it was for justice to be done.

" Official voting disk "

▲ The ballots were mass-produced and have a rough-and-ready look. But they had their part to play in a well-ordered system.

▶ These inscribed *pinakia* (metal tickets) and the bronze ball from a *kleroterion* (voting machine) were used in the random selection of juries for Athens's courts.

Doing Your Duty

Democracy brings responsibilities as well as rights. Not only was the Athenian citizen expected to play his part in political discussions and making decisions, but his help was also needed in the administration of the law.

An Athenian jury was far larger than anything you would expect to see in a modern American courthouse, and might easily have two hundred members, or even more.

Being a good citizen of Athens was practically a full-time job. This is one reason why it was so important that the city had such a big population of foreigners and slaves.

Human nature being what it is, citizens were not always eager to do their duty. Rotas had to be drawn up so that there would always be jurors available. The danger of a strict rota, though, was that it would become too easy to predict who would be on the jury for a particular case. Those individuals would then be vulnerable to threats or open to bribes.

Random Selection

To avoid this possibility, big blocks of two thousand citizens at a time were chosen, drawing on all of the city's ten electoral tribes. Then on the day of the trial, selections were made within these blocks at random. Each potential juror had a *pinakia* (metal ticket) inscribed with his name. All of these were inserted into a special machine, called the *kleroterion*. A funnel at the top was filled with black and white balls, which fed into a tube underneath in random order. Turning a crank at the bottom of this tube released a ball. Each time someone's *pinakia* was pulled out, the crank was turned and another ball was released. If the ball was black, that juror was sent home. If it was white he was sworn in to serve on the jury.

▼ Part of a *kleroterion*: once the *pinakia* had been inserted into the slots, there was no way of knowing whose name was on each one.

AN ENEMY OF THE PEOPLE

IT TOOK SECONDS TO SCRATCH A MAN'S NAME UPON AN ATHENIAN OSTRACON (A PIECE OF BROKEN POTTERY), BUT THE RESULTS COULD HAVE TRAGIC CONSEQUENCES FOR HIS LIFE.

It might be said that modern democracy is really not all that democratic. Presidential elections are held just once every four years. Each elector has his or her single vote, but the election's winner has all the power. A modern administration will make thousands of decisions, great and small.

Athenian democracy had many limitations. It depended on the labor of slaves, and it excluded women, to name just two. But in a way we can hardly imagine now, it gave its ordinary electors a say in the day-to-day decisions of the state.

▼ Athenians argue a case in the city square. Crowds have their own psychology and ostracism was a highly public process. It was easy for popular resentment to develop into mass hysteria as it did against Themistocles.

THE TRANSLATION

The ostracon's message is stark: the citizen has cast his vote against Themistocles. The happiness of the individual is nothing when weighed against the will of the people.

" Themistocles – Neokleos ... "

◀ Themistocles became so unpopular that archaeologists at work in the ruins of ancient Athens have frequently found ostracons inscribed with his name.

37

DID YOU KNOW?

Unable to return to Athens, Themistocles finally found a welcome with his former Persian enemies. Xerxes's son, Artaxerxes I (reigned from 465 to 424 BCE), made him governor of Magnesia in Asia Minor (modern Turkey). Themistocles served the emperor loyally until his death in Magnesia in 459 BCE.

But people power also had a vicious streak. When a public figure fell out of favor, he might be expelled from Athens altogether, in a process known as ostracism. This involved the people scratching the name of the man they wanted to get rid of onto an ostracon. The Greeks used these for jotting down notes, the same way we might use scraps of paper. Below the name, they had to write the name of the deme (the electoral tribe or division) he came from. In this case, the man was Themistocles (524–459 BCE), and he belonged to the Prearrhus deme.

The ostracons were counted, and if there were enough votes, the victim was ostracized. He had to leave the city, and could not come back for ten years. If he tried to return, he would be put to death.

◀ Masterminded by Themistocles, the Athenians' victory at Salamis in 480 BCE undoubtedly saved their city from complete destruction by the Persians.

An Ungrateful Electorate

The case of Themistocles shows how hard it could be to please the electorate. Once, he had been the hero of Athens in its darkest days. In 490 BCE at Marathon he had helped inspire Athens's famous victory over the invasion force of the Persian emperor, Darius I (reigned from 522 to 486 BCE). Then, when others had wanted Athens to sit back and enjoy its triumph, Themistocles had argued

▲ With his ashes placed in an elegant amphora (jar), his remaining friends lay Themistocles to rest in a romantic painting by the Italian artist Giuseppi Bossi (1771–1815).

tirelessly for the city to keep building up its defensive strength. Though most people wanted the money spent on spectacular public buildings, Themistocles urged the Athenians to build more warships, and construct a fortified wall around Piraeus, the port of Athens. Fortunately the Athenians were persuaded, because in 480 BCE the son of Darius, Xerxes (reigned from 486 to 465 BCE), attacked. His 100,000 men had swept through countryside beyond Athens until they were massed outside the city itself.

Themistocles stayed calm. His fleet set a trap for the Persian ships, luring them into the strait of Salamis. They were trapped there, and then smashed by the Athenian ships. Without naval support, Xerxes's army had to withdraw and the invasion threat ended.

Themistocles was rightly the hero of the hour, but he was in no mood for celebration. He insisted that the Athenians should be building up their defenses still further. The invading Persians had reduced the monuments of the acropolis to ruins, but Themistocles did not want to rebuild them. He wanted them to be left as they were, as a warning of the threats that Athens faced.

A Savior Scorned

Because of his attitude, the Athenians resented Themistocles, and in 471 BCE they ostracized him. So great was their hatred that he was not allowed to return, even when his ten-year exile was up.

THE PRICE OF FREEDOM

SCRIBBLES ON THE WALL OF APOLLO'S TEMPLE AT DELPHI BEAR WITNESS TO THE FREEING OF SLAVES, WHO WERE RELEASED FROM SLAVERY BY BEING SOLD TO THE GOD HIMSELF.

The whole wall is covered with scrawls. More and more were added through the early centuries BCE. It is an untidy sight and yet an inspiring one, as each of these inscriptions meant freedom for some man or woman.

This was the formula the Greeks used when they were releasing people from slavery. The idea that the slave might have a right to his or her own freedom was not really imaginable to them. It did not occur to them that slaves could simply be freed on their own account. Instead, the ancient Greeks went through the ritual of selling a human slave to the god Apollo, as though he were another human owner.

Strict Conditions

The owners of slaves were not necessarily acting out of pure generosity. While some may well have freed their slaves on sentimental grounds, most of these slaves were released under strict conditions. Apollo's price—the money with which the god supposedly paid for the slave—would have to be paid by the former slave from his or her earnings as a free worker.

◀ In Homer's epic, the *Iliad*, the hero Achilles falls in love with the slave girl Briseis. Here she serves Achilles's aged tutor, Phoenix.

THE TRANSLATION

66 At a price of three and a half silver minas, Pythian Apollo bought a Roman-born woman slave named Nicaea from Sosibius, with a view to securing her liberty. The seller under the law was Eumnastos of Amphissa. He has received his money and the purchase was carried out in the name of Apollo, so the slave could have her freedom...

Telon and Cleto, with the agreement of their son Straton, sold Pythian Apollo a male slave named Sosus, a Cappadocian by birth, at a price of three silver minas. Sosus commissioned the god to handle the sale on the condition that he should have his freedom guaranteed, so that no one might be able to claim ownership of him for all time... **99**

▼ Sold to Apollo: The graffiti on the walls of Apollo's temple bear witness to the freeing of hundreds of Greek slaves over several centuries.

And many slaves were set free only as long as they promised to serve their former owner until his or her death. That was how it was with "a male Galatian slave named Maiphatas and a female Illyrian slave called Ammia." Their master Critodamus gave them their freedom, but they had to stay with him "for as long as he should live, doing whatever he should order them; if they should leave him or refuse to

▼ Today the Temple of Apollo in Delphi is a dramatic ruin. The destinies of many suffering slaves were decided here in ancient times.

do his bidding, this sale will be considered canceled."

Cruel Calculations

This was a cunning scheme on the master's part because the agreement forced the slave to be on his or her best behavior if he or she ultimately wanted to be set free. It also meant that when he or she died, the slave would be alone, and Critodamus's family would have no obligation to keep a freed slave through their old age. Even so, it seems likely that Maiphatas and Ammia still looked forward to receiving their freedom, however long they had to toil until that day came.

Democratic Double Standard

The liberty-loving Greeks never considered that owning other people might be wrong. Many slaves had been captured in wars of long ago, and their descendants had remained in slavery ever since. New slaves were also constantly being shipped in from colonies overseas.

According to the Greek philosopher Aristotle (384–322 BCE), it was not even considered kind to allow barbarians their freedom. They were naturally slaves, incapable of understanding freedom, he believed, and needed a master's guidance.

DID YOU KNOW?

A census conducted in the fourth century BCE revealed that there were 400,000 slaves in Athens and Attica (the area of countryside around the city). That adds up to twenty slaves for every free citizen.

TRIBUTE TO A TEACHER

THE INSCRIPTION IS ONLY A FRAGMENT, BUT IT IS ENOUGH TO REMIND US OF THE BOND BETWEEN TWO OF THE MOST EXTRAORDINARY FIGURES OF ANCIENT TIMES.

At one time, it appears, the stone was a herm (a flat slab with a sculpted human head on top). It was uncovered during excavations of the stoa (covered walkway) of Attalos, on the eastern side of the agora. But that stoa was not built until the second century BCE, and this sculpture must have been made a century before that.

The herm's head is missing, but the inscription leaves no doubt as to whom it was. Aristotle (384–322 BCE) was not just one of the greatest philosophers of his age, he was also one of the greatest thinkers of all time. As for Alexander (356–323 BCE), he must have dedicated this monument in the early 330s BCE, before he set off on one of the greatest campaigns of military conquest the world has seen.

Fellow Countrymen

Aristotle and Alexander went back a long way. Both came from Macedon, a rugged, mountainous kingdom in the north of Greece. The philosopher's father was court doctor to King Amyntas III (reigned from 392 to 370 BCE), the father of Philip II of Macedon (reigned from 359 to 336 BCE). Philip was Alexander's father.

◄ Alexander the Great was destined to conquer much of the known world, but he stood in awe of his great teacher, Aristotle.

THE TRANSLATION

Alexander's admiration and affection for his old teacher are clear. But it may also be that, as a Macedonian (who were considered barbarians by the Greeks), he wanted to advertize his own respect for the intellectual life.

66 Alexander set up this portrait of the divine Aristotle, son of Nichomachos, fountain of all wisdom... **99**

◀ Aristotle's importance was already clear in his own age. Alexander still had much to prove when he dedicated this herma to his teacher.

45

Macedon was a remote and backward place, so it is not surprising that Aristotle took himself off to Athens as soon as he could. He stayed there for twenty years.

New Ways of Thinking

It was an exciting time for philosophy. Aristotle studied under Plato (429–347 BCE), who was developing ideas that were to influence philosophy for many centuries to come. Aristotle, as his student, was developing his own

approach. He disagreed completely with just about everything Plato said. He thought there was no point in wondering what lay beyond reality—we had to do what we could with the way things were. To his way of thinking, we can only know what we can actually perceive with our own senses and what we can test by direct observation.

These insights obviously make Aristotle the founder of scientific thought, but he applied his methods to other subjects, too. He had theories about everything from psychology to politics. But he always believed in starting out from what was. For example, when he wrote about the theory of tragedy, he only discussed plays he himself had actually seen, and

▼ The first philosophers, like Socrates, made a living by giving public classes in Athens's stoai, which was filled with noise and bustle.

46

▶ Plato and Aristotle argue things out in a carving from a medieval church. The debate they began has continued in philosophy to this day.

when he wrote about politics, he drew on examples from actual states.

Revolutionizing the way people think can be dangerous. Plato's teacher, Socrates (c. 469–399 BCE), was accused of being a bad influence on Athenian youth, and was forced to commit suicide. And around 346 BCE, Aristotle fell foul of powerful people in Athens. He fled to Macedonia where the new king, Philip II, asked him to take charge of his son's education. Aristotle tutored Alexander for six or seven years. By the end of that time, things had quietened down in Athens, while Alexander was too grown-up to need his help, so Aristotle headed south again to take up his old teaching life in Athens.

ALEXANDER'S TEMPLE

IN 334 BCE ALEXANDER THE GREAT CELEBRATED HIS FIRST VICTORIES OVER THE PERSIANS BY DEDICATING A TEMPLE TO THE GODDESS ATHENA IN ASIA MINOR.

As a teenager, Alexander (356–323 BCE) notoriously complained that his father, Philip II (reigned from 359 to 336 BCE), had conquered too much territory. Soon, he said, there would not be enough world left for him. But he quickly proved himself wrong. He had only just succeeded his father in 336 BCE before he decided to take on the might of Persia. He was still only nineteen years old.

▼ At the Battle of Granicus (334 BCE) Alexander's army outnumbered Persian forces by a huge number, yet Alexander presented it as a sensational victory.

Early in 334 BCE he led an invasion force across the Dardanelles. These are the straits between the far northeast of Greece and Asia Minor (modern Turkey). He had just over 40,000 men. A small party of Persians advanced to meet them on the banks of the Granicus River, and Alexander's army defeated them with ease. Alexander proclaimed it a great victory. He was exaggerating, but he understood the importance of establishing himself by managing his image and boasting about his accomplishments.

THE TRANSLATION

WHAT DOES IT MEAN?
Alexander presents himself as a champion of Greek values. Ironically, his gift of money ran out, and the temple had to be completed by the citizens of Priene much later.

" King Alexander dedicated the temple to Athena Polias. "

◄ Alexander's temple was supposedly an offering to the goddess Athena and to Greece, but he really built it to reinforce his own fame.

49

This was why he was so careful to present himself as a Greek. In fact, as a Macedonian, the Greeks were likely to see him as a barbarian outsider, especially because his father Philip II had come to the Greek cities as a conqueror. But the old Greek colonies of western Anatolia had been under Persian rule for generations, so Alexander was able to reinvent himself as representative of Greek culture here. That way, he could rely on being welcomed as a liberator as he inflicted defeat after defeat on the Persians.

Alexander the Greek

No city was more Greek than Priene, despite its location in Ionia, in western Turkey. A wealthy seaport, it had been a Greek colony for centuries. The estuary by which it stood was blocked with sand and mud, so a splendid new showcase city was being built inland. A site had been found on raised ground to display the treasures of the city to the best possible advantage. The city was laid out following a system devised by Hippodamus of Miletus (498–408 BCE). He was a master planner of orderly and beautiful cities, as opposed to the confusing and intricate older cities of that time, such as Athens.

It is easy to see why Alexander would want to associate himself with Priene. Even by Greek standards, Priene was beautiful, and was highly pleasing to the eye in its balanced proportions. Alexander's temple sat neatly in the overall layout of the city. Athena Polias (Athena of the City) was the patron goddess of Athens, but she was also goddess of the Greek polis (city-state). So she represented all the values Alexander hoped to have associated with his name.

Chameleon King

Alexander went on to conquer a vast empire, first striking south into Egypt and then pushing eastward to take Persia. He defeated Darius III (reigned from 336 to 330 BCE) at the Battle of Issus, in 333 BCE. Then he smashed the emperor's forces finally at Gaugamela, in modern-day Iraq, in 331 BCE.

He quickly made himself master of the Persian Empire, which extended through much of western and central Asia. By now, Alexander had left his Greek phase well behind him. Now in Persia, he took on many of the trappings the emperors there had used. In Egypt, he made himself a pharaoh in the traditional way, meaning he was not just a ruler but also a god. He finally fell ill and died in Babylon in 323 BCE, the greatest conqueror the world had seen.

▲ Priene was rocked by a succession of earthquakes in the centuries after its construction. Even now, though, its spectacular beauty can still be seen.

THE PARIAN MARBLE

THIS MYSTERIOUS MARBLE STELA IS INSCRIBED WITH A CHRONOLOGICAL TABLE THAT COVERS MORE THAN A THOUSAND YEARS. HISTORICAL EVENTS APPEAR SIDE BY SIDE WITH MYTH.

The island of Paros has been celebrated since ancient times for the quality of its stone, where the so-called "Parian marble" was considered to be the finest in the world. But the Parian Marble is famous, too. Ever since its discovery three hundred years ago, it has fascinated historians who study ancient times.

Hard Facts

The Parian Marble has also bewildered historians, because it is hard to tell whether its inscription is meant to be serious or is some kind of elaborate ancient joke. It is a chronological table that sets out the whole sweep of Greek history right up to the moment when it was carved, up to about 299 BCE. Many of the dates it gives

agree with what is known from other sources. For example, it says that in 561 BCE, the tyrant Peisistratos seized power in Athens. Historians know that

THE TRANSLATION

❝ 1582: Cecrops I is king in Athens.

1521: King Hellen I of Phtiosis gives the name Hellenes to the Greek people and inaugurates the Panathenaian Games.

1500: Hyagnis, father of Marsyas, invented the flute...

▲ This was among the first Greek inscriptions to be translated in modern times. Even now, it is hard to think of a stranger one.

1259: Theseus became king of Athens and brought the twelve townships into one, giving them government and democracy...

1218: The Trojan War begins...

1209: The Fall of Troy...

c. 790: Archias, son of Eagetus, the tenth in line of descent from Temenus, led a party of colonists from Corinth to found Syracuse ... when Aeschylus, king of Athens, was in the twenty-first year of his reign...

683: The annual archonship [office of chief magistrate] was set up...

644: Terpander of Lesbos, son of Derdenes, found a new way of playing the lyre, and modified the old style. Dropides was archon of Athens...

581: The competition for the wreath was reintroduced at Delphi.

561: Peisistratos the Tyrant seized power in Athens.

490: The Athenians fought the Persians at Marathon ... and won the battle... ❞

53

▲ The Parian Marble lists legends, like that of the Trojan War (shown here), alongside real historical events. In the maker's mind, no difference apparently existed.

this is true, just as they know that the inscription is correct when it says that the Greeks defeated the invading Persians at the Battle of Marathon in 490 BCE.

Impossible Fictions

But alongside factual events like this, the table lists what are obviously mythical tales. It makes no distinction between what are simply stories and what are true histories.

While the story of Deucalion's flood (the equivalent of Noah's biblical flood in the Greek myths) is interesting and enjoyable to read about, it is perplexing that the story is listed here as being part of history, and dated precisely to 1529 BCE.

The invention of the flute is pinned down to the exact year of 1500 BCE, yet from archaeological evidence, it is

▲ Was the Earl of Arundel ahead of his time or far, far behind it? His interest in the ancient Greeks was thought very odd by other Englishmen of the seventeenth century.

known that the flute, one of the earliest musical instruments, evolved over many centuries.

Once you get used to the idea that the Parian Marble is presenting a mixture of fact and fiction, it comes as no real surprise to be confidently told that in 1255 BCE Athens came under attack from Amazons, a race of wild warrior women. Nor is it a shock to be given exact dates (1218–1209 BCE) for the Trojan War, which was actually only a myth.

DELPHIC DENIAL

IN 279 BCE A BAND OF CELTIC WARRIORS SACKED THE CELEBRATED SHRINE AT DELPHI. BUT THE GREEKS WERE RELUCTANT TO ACKNOWLEDGE THAT IT HAD EVEN HAPPENED.

Delphi is in the heart of Greece, just to the north of the Gulf of Corinth. In Greek eyes, that made it the center of the world. A peculiarly shaped stone here seemed to them to look like a person's navel, so they called it omphalos (navel of the earth). This was a holy place. It was under the spiritual protection of the priestesses of Apollo, who had a temple dedicated to him just nearby.

▶ A king is depicted consulting the Oracle of Delphi on this decorated plate. For the sake of the design, she is portrayed as being behind a wall, not below the ground.

THE TRANSLATION

WHAT DOES IT MEAN?

As late as the third century BCE, and even in outlying areas of the Greek world, people still felt a close kinship with Greece and its oldest traditions.

❝ Of the barbarians who launched an invasion of Greece and attacked the shrine at Delphi, we hear that those who attacked the temple were punished both by the gods and the men of that place, who came to save the shrine when they realized it was under assault. The temple has been saved and decorated with the captured weapons of its attackers, the rest having been destroyed in further fighting with the Greeks. This is to show the rejoicing of the people at this great victory and the sacrifices they have offered to the god in thanks for his intervention in saving the temple, its precincts, and indeed the whole of Greece. **❞**

▼ A memorial to Delphi found on the island of Cos. Delphi was meant to be sacred for all Greeks, whether they lived in Greece itself, or on an offshore island like Cos.

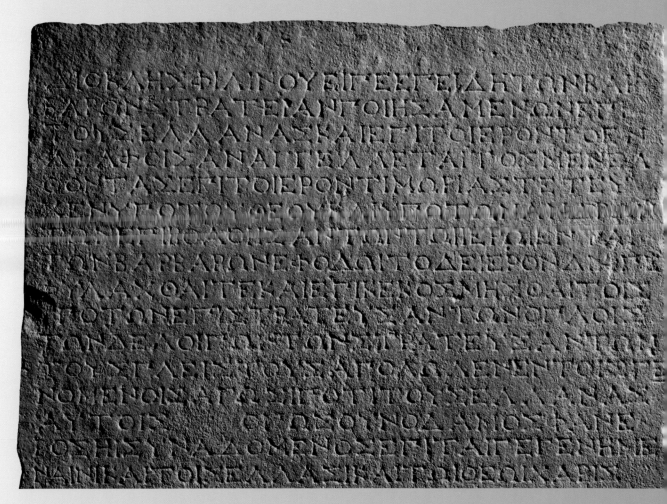

There was a crack in the rocks below the omphalos, and a hollow chamber underneath. At key moments, one priestess, known as the Pythia, would go down into this cave. There she would chant out her prophecies of what was to come. To listeners above, her voice seemed to be issuing from the earth. Her pronouncements sounded like mad ravings, but were believed to hold important wisdom. They were regarded as religious riddles to be solved.

Primitive Instincts

Even in ancient times this was already an ancient tradition, and it shows us a different side of the Greeks from the one we are used to. We are always hearing that the Greeks prepared the way for modern science and philosophy. In honor of Athena, Apollo, and the other deities, the Greeks built wonderful temples and created beautiful vases. In ancient Greece, religion and human advancement went hand in hand.

Although this is true, it is not the whole story. The Greeks also lived in a world in which war was an ever-present threat. At any time, the crops could fail and

▶ A horse leaps over a wild boar on this Celtic coin from the first century BCE. The image symbolizes the strength and warlike courage of the Celts.

bring terrible famine. However much faith they had in their new ways of thinking, they could not quite let go of their older, more primitive customs.

▲ The people of Cos felt that they were every bit as Greek as the people on the mainland. The cities and temples they built were the same as any you might find anywhere in Greece.

An Uncomfortable Truth

One tradition that seems to be as old as humanity itself is that of ignoring unwelcome truths. That is what happened when the Celtic chieftain Brennos (died 279 BCE) led a huge war party over the mountains from central Europe into Greece. Most modern historians agree that Brennos and his warriors sacked the shrine at Delphi.

The Greeks themselves, though, insist that they had been beaten off. The gods came to the rescue, they say. The Greeks were so convincing in their claim that communities across the country—like this one, on the island of Cos—put up memorials, thanking the gods for their assistance. The Celts, for their part, had a religious taboo against writing of any sort, so there are no inscriptions to give their side of their story.

GLOSSARY

artifact—An object made for a practical purpose by a craftsman that often has artistic qualities.

backwater—A place that is isolated or backward.

barbarian—Someone who (in the opinion of the speaker) is uncivilized. The word is said to come from the Greek and Roman view that the peoples they conquered talked a nonsense language that sounded, to their ears, like "Ba-ba-ba."

bronze—A metal made mainly of copper, but with tin mixed in for extra hardness. On its own, copper was found to be too soft to make usable tools or weapons.

Bronze Age—The period in which people had mastered the skills and technology of working in bronze, but not iron. In Greece, the Bronze Age lasted from about 1600 to 900 BCE.

catastrophe—A violent and destructive event.

census—A government count of the population of a place.

citadel—A fortified stronghold at the center of an ancient city. The city's rulers could retreat into it if the city came under attack.

civic—Relating to a society, or in the case of the Greeks, to a city-state.

colony—A settlement established by people from one country in another. It might be merely a trading outpost, or a way of establishing control over a larger territory.

democracy—From the Greek words *demos* (people) and *cracia* (rule). To use President Abraham Lincoln's famous phrase, democracy is "government of the people, by the people, for the people."

elite—A small group considered to be above everyone else in status.

epic—A long story, often told in poetry, about great heroes and their adventures.

graffiti—Writing or drawing on a wall or public place.

incomprehensible—Something that cannot be understood.

Iron Age—The period in which people learned to work with iron. Iron is a much more difficult metal to work than bronze, but it is also much harder and more durable. In Greece, the Iron Age began around the ninth century BCE.

militaristic—Dedicated to military discipline and war. Just about all civilizations have had armies, but some cultures (such as Sparta) make war the main measure of personal honor and patriotic pride.

nouns—The names given to a thing or subject.

oracle—A person or place that can foretell what will happen in the future. In ancient Greece, priestesses at sacred sites were thought to reveal the hidden words of the gods.

oral tradition—Stories, songs, poems, or knowledge handed down from generation to generation by word of mouth, rather than in written form.

ostracism—Banishing someone from a place by popular vote.

pastoral—A poem that celebrates the peace and harmony of life in the country among shepherds and shepherdesses, far away from the noise and bustle of the city.

rota—An order or list of something or of a group of people.

sack—To plunder and destroy a settlement, temple, or city.

satire—Humor that makes a serious point by poking fun at the way a society lives, or the way it is ruled.

scribe—Someone whose profession it is to write. In ancient civilizations the majority of the people were unable to read or write, so the scribes had an important position in the state.

Semitic—Part of a group of peoples with similar languages who originate from the Middle East and include the Hebrews and Arabs.

shrine—Any place or building that is holy.

stela—A standing stone monument that is inscribed with words or pictures (or both).

subject—Someone who is under the authority or the dominance of another.

taboo—A very strong religious or social ban.

tithe—A measure of one-tenth of what a family or community has produced, given up as a tax to the authorities.

tyrant—A ruler who has complete power and governs on the basis of his or her own personal desires.

TIMELINE OF GREECE

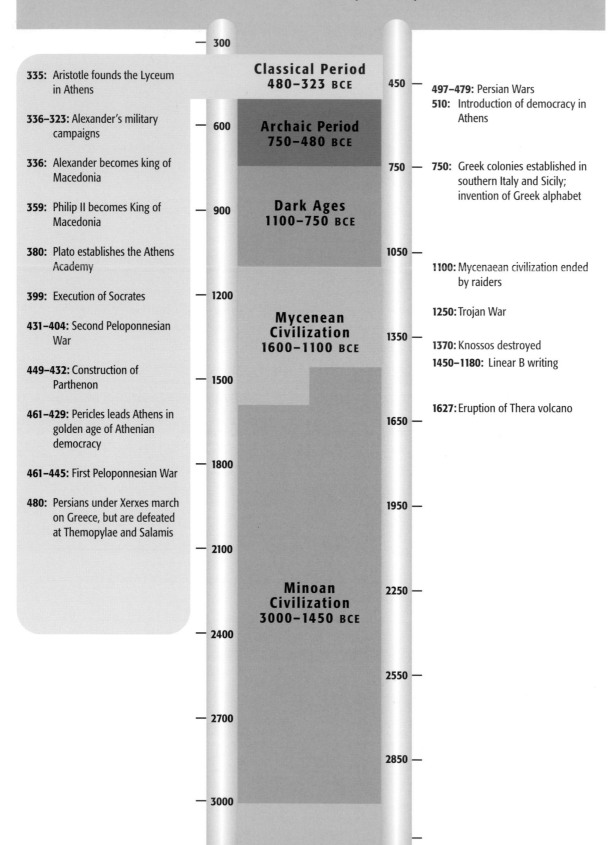

335: Aristotle founds the Lyceum in Athens

336–323: Alexander's military campaigns

336: Alexander becomes king of Macedonia

359: Philip II becomes King of Macedonia

380: Plato establishes the Athens Academy

399: Execution of Socrates

431–404: Second Peloponnesian War

449–432: Construction of Parthenon

461–429: Pericles leads Athens in golden age of Athenian democracy

461–445: First Peloponnesian War

480: Persians under Xerxes march on Greece, but are defeated at Themopylae and Salamis

— 300

Classical Period
480–323 BCE

— 600

Archaic Period
750–480 BCE

— 900

Dark Ages
1100–750 BCE

— 1200

Mycenean Civilization
1600–1100 BCE

— 1500

— 1800

— 2100

Minoan Civilization
3000–1450 BCE

— 2400

— 2700

— 3000

450

497–479: Persian Wars
510: Introduction of democracy in Athens

750

750: Greek colonies established in southern Italy and Sicily; invention of Greek alphabet

1050

1100: Mycenaean civilization ended by raiders

1250: Trojan War

1350

1370: Knossos destroyed
1450–1180: Linear B writing

1627: Eruption of Thera volcano

1650 —

1950 —

2250 —

2550 —

2850 —

FURTHER INFORMATION

BOOKS

Claybourne, Anna. *Ancient Greece* (Time Travel Guides). Chicago: Heinemann-Raintree, 2007.

Kuhtz, Cleo, and Hazel Mary Martell. *Ancient Greek Civilization* (Ancient Civilizations and Their Myths and Legends). New York: Rosen Publishing, 2009.

Pearson, Anne. *Ancient Greece* (DK Eyewitness Books). New York: DK Children, 2007.

Schomp, Virginia. *The Ancient Greeks* (Myths of the World). New York: Marshall Cavendish, 2008.

WEBSITES

The British Museum: Ancient Greece—www.britishmuseum.org/explore/world_cultures/europe/ancient_greece.aspx

History for Kids: Ancient Greece—www.historyforkids.org/learn/greeks

NOVA: Secrets of the Parthenon—www.pbs.org/wgbh/nova/parthenon/hurwit.html

Odyssey Online: Greece—www.carlos.emory.edu/ODYSSEY/GREECE/welcome.html

THE AUTHOR

Michael Kerrigan has written dozens of books for children and young adults over the last twenty years. He is the author of *The Ancients in Their Own Words* (2008), *A Dark History: The Roman Emperors* (2008), and *Ancient Greece and the Mediterranean* (part of the BBC Ancient Civilizations series). He also works as a columnist, book reviewer, and feature writer for publications including the *Scotsman* and the *Times Literary Supplement*. He lives in Edinburgh, Scotland.

INDEX